Women of UnShakable Faith

31-Day Devotional for Strength, Purpose & Influence

Gerard Assey

Women of UnShakable Faith:
31-Day Devotional for
Strength, Purpose & Influence
By
Gerard Assey

Published by:
Gerard Assey
19/18, Palli Arasan Street
Anna Nagar East
Chennai - 600 102

ISBN: 978-81-985691-0-3

Table of Contents

Preface

FAITH & PURPOSE IN THE WORKPLACE

- ✓ DAY 1: Lois & Eunice – Generational Faithfulness
(Passing Down Faith While Managing Home and Work)
- ✓ DAY 2: Deborah – The Working Woman Who Led a Nation
(Balancing Leadership, Wisdom, and Faith)
- ✓ DAY 3: Lydia – The Entrepreneur Who Supported Ministry
(Excelling in Business While Honoring God)
- ✓ DAY 4: Esther – Courage in the Corporate World
(Taking Bold Steps in a Challenging Workplace)
- ✓ DAY 5: Huldah – A Woman of Wisdom in a Male-Dominated World
(Being a Voice of Knowledge and Discernment)
- ✓ DAY 6: Priscilla – Balancing Work, Ministry & Marriage
(Supporting Family While Making an Impact)
- ✓ DAY 7: Sarah – Trusting God's Timing
(Handling Workplace Delays and Personal Disappointments)

STRENGTH FOR DAILY CHALLENGES

- ✓ DAY 8: Hannah – Praying Through Workplace Struggles
(Finding Strength Through Prayer in Stressful Times)

- ✓ DAY 9: Ruth – Diligence & Hard Work (Staying Dedicated Despite Difficult Circumstances)
- ✓ DAY 10: Martha – Managing Work Without Losing Focus on God (Learning to Balance Work and Spiritual Priorities)
- ✓ DAY 11: Jochebed – Raising Children While Trusting God (Managing Motherhood and Work Without Fear)
- ✓ DAY 12: Mary, Mother of Jesus – Embracing a Divine Calling (Handling Unexpected Life Changes While Working)
- ✓ DAY 13: The Proverbs 31 Woman – Excellence in Every Role (Being a Role Model at Work and Home)
- ✓ DAY 14: Zipporah – Protecting Family Values in a Busy Life (Ensuring Spiritual Leadership at Home)

OVERCOMING CHALLENGES WITH GRACE

- ✓ DAY 15: Rahab – Overcoming a Bad Reputation & Finding Purpose (Rising Above Past Mistakes and Succeeding)
- ✓ DAY 16: Mary & Martha – Work vs. Worship (Choosing What Truly Matters in a Busy Schedule)
- ✓ DAY 17: Eve – Learning from Mistakes (Avoiding Workplace Temptations and Distractions)
- ✓ DAY 18: Tamar – Justice for the Voiceless (Standing Strong When Wronged in the Workplace)

TRUSTING GOD AND TAKING ACTION

- ✓ DAY 19: Anna the Prophetess – Faithfulness in the Waiting
  (Trusting God's Promises Through Long Seasons)
- ✓ DAY 20: Abigail – Wisdom & Peacemaking in Workplace Conflict
  (Managing Difficult People with Grace)
- ✓ DAY 21: Jael – Stepping Up When Others Won't
  (Seizing Opportunities with Boldness)

BUILDING A LEGACY OF FAITH

- ✓ DAY 22: Elizabeth – Encouraging Others While Waiting on God
  (Uplifting Coworkers While Waiting for Personal Breakthroughs)
- ✓ DAY 23: The Shunammite Woman – Radical Generosity & Trust in God
  (Investing in the Lives of Others While Working)
- ✓ DAY 24: Phoebe – Serving While Leading
  (Being a Leader and a Servant at the Same Time)
- ✓ DAY 25: Miriam – Leading Women in Worship & Work
  (Leading with Grace and Humility)

FAITH & FINANCES

- ✓ DAY 26: The Widow of Zarephath – Trusting God in Financial Crisis
  (Relying on God in Difficult Financial Situations)

- ✓ DAY 27: Susanna – Using Resources to Support God's Work
(Financial Stewardship and Generosity)

FAITH IN ACTION

- ✓ DAY 28: The Canaanite Woman – Bold Faith in the Face of Rejection
(Pushing Forward Despite Challenges at Work)
- ✓ DAY 29: Dorcas (Tabitha) – Making an Impact Through Good Works
(Using Skills to Bless Others While Working)

FAITH IN ACTION AND INFLUENCE

- ✓ DAY 30: Joanna – A Woman of Influence in the Workplace
(Being a Godly Influence in a Secular Workplace)
- ✓ DAY 31: YOU – Walking in Unshakable Faith Every Day
(Living Out Your Calling as a Woman of God)

Conclusion
About the Author

Preface

Welcome to '**Women of Unshakable Faith: *31-Day Devotional for Strength, Purpose, and Influence*'**. Whether you are an entrepreneur, a corporate professional, a teacher, a healthcare worker, a homemaker, or serving in any other role, this devotional is for you. As a woman of faith, you are called to balance multiple responsibilities—work, family, relationships, and spiritual growth. Some days, it may feel overwhelming. Other times, you may question if your faith truly makes a difference in your workplace and daily life.

But here's the truth: God has placed you exactly where you are for a purpose. He has equipped you with unique gifts, wisdom, and strength to influence those around you, whether through leadership, service, kindness, or resilience. The Bible is full of inspiring stories of women who faced challenges, overcame adversity, and lived out their faith in ways that changed history. This devotional brings their journeys to life, helping you apply their lessons to your own.

Why This Devotional?

This 31-day journey is designed to:

- ✓ *Strengthen Your Faith – Through the examples of biblical women, you will see how God works through every season, challenge, and opportunity in your life.*
- ✓ *Encourage You in Your Work – Whether you are facing workplace struggles, leadership challenges, financial difficulties, or time*

management concerns, this devotional offers practical insights to keep your focus on God.

- ✓ *Help You Find Purpose – Each story will remind you that no job is too small, no role too insignificant when surrendered to God's will.*
- ✓ *Empower You to Influence – As a working woman of faith, your impact extends beyond your job title. This devotional will inspire you to bring God's love and wisdom into every space you enter.*

How to Use This Devotional

- ✓ *Each day focuses on one remarkable woman from the Bible, offering: Scripture – A passage that highlights her story and God's message.*
- ✓ *Devotional Story – A powerful, real-life scenario that connects biblical truth to modern work-life challenges.*
- ✓ *Lesson Learned – A reflection on how her story applies to your faith journey.*
- ✓ *Reflection Questions – Designed to help you think deeply and personally about the topic.*
- ✓ *Action Plan for the Day – A practical step to apply what you've learned in your daily work and life.*
- ✓ *Prayer – A short but powerful prayer to seek God's guidance and strength.*

You can use this devotional in different ways:

- ✓ *Morning Inspiration: Start your day with a short but powerful reflection, inviting God into your work and plans.*
- ✓ *Evening Reflection: Wind down by meditating on what God has taught you and how you can apply it tomorrow.*

- ✓ *Group Study: This devotional can also be used in small groups, Bible studies, or workplace fellowships. Share insights and encourage one another!*

You Are Called for Such a Time as This!

Sister, you are not just another worker, wife, mother, or leader—you are a daughter of the King, placed here for a divine purpose. As you go through this devotional, I pray that your faith will be strengthened, your confidence in God will grow, and your influence in your workplace and home will shine brightly.

May this journey help you become a Woman of Unshakable Faith!
With love and prayers,

FAITH & PURPOSE IN THE WORKPLACE

DAY 1:
Lois & Eunice – Generational Faithfulness
(Passing Down Faith While Managing Home and Work)

Scripture:
"I am reminded of your sincere faith, which first lived in your grandmother Lois and in your mother Eunice and, I am persuaded, now lives in you also." – **2 Timothy 1:5 (NIV)**

Devotional Story:
The alarm clock buzzed, and Rachel groggily reached over to turn it off. It was another busy day—a morning meeting with her team, deadlines to meet, and a long list of emails to respond to. But before any of that, she had one non-negotiable appointment: morning prayers with her 10-year-old daughter, Lily.
Rachel's own mother, Margaret, had done the same when Rachel was growing up. No matter how busy life got, Margaret always found time to pray with her children, read Bible stories at bedtime, and show them how faith intertwined with everyday life. Now, as a working mother juggling spreadsheets and school lunches, Rachel often wondered, *Am I doing enough to pass my faith down?*
She thought about Lois and Eunice, two ordinary yet extraordinary women in the Bible. They weren't queens, warriors, or prophets—they were simply a mother and a grandmother who raised Timothy, a man who became a powerful leader in the early

church. Their names were not known for great exploits, but their faith left a lasting legacy. They raised a boy who would one day stand beside the Apostle Paul and carry the Gospel forward.

Rachel smiled as Lily recited her memory verse for the week. *Yes, deadlines are important. Meetings matter. But this? This is eternal work.*

Lesson Learned:

In today's fast-paced world, it's easy to believe that passing down faith requires grand gestures—long sermons, perfect family devotions, or deep theological knowledge. But Lois and Eunice remind us that faith is best transferred through daily, consistent actions.

It happens in:

- ✓ The prayers whispered over your children before bed.
- ✓ The way you react when things go wrong at work.
- ✓ The small moments when you teach them to trust God.

Faith is not just taught; it is caught—in the way you live, love, and lead.

Reflection Questions:

1. *In what small ways can you integrate faith into your daily work and home life?*
2. *Who has been a spiritual mentor in your life, and how have they influenced your faith?*
3. *How can you be intentional in passing your faith to the next generation?*

Action Plan for the Day:

- ✓ Pray for someone younger in your workplace or family today. Ask God to help you be a Lois or Eunice to them.
- ✓ Choose one simple way to share your faith today—whether through a kind word, a Bible verse, or an act of generosity.
- ✓ If you have children, set aside five minutes to talk to them about something God has done in your life.

Prayer:

Heavenly Father, thank You for the example of Lois and Eunice. Help me to live out my faith in such a way that it becomes a lasting legacy for those around me. Let my words, actions, and decisions reflect Your love and truth. Teach me to balance my work, my home, and my calling to nurture faith in others. In Jesus' Name, Amen.

DAY 2:
Deborah – The Working Woman Who Led a Nation
(Balancing Leadership, Wisdom, and Faith)

Scripture:
"Now Deborah, a prophet, the wife of Lappidoth, was leading Israel at that time. She held court under the Palm of Deborah between Ramah and Bethel in the hill country of Ephraim, and the Israelites went up to her to have their disputes decided." – **Judges 4:4-5 (NIV)**

Devotional Story:
Monica stared at the overflowing email inbox and sighed. As a senior manager in a fast-growing company, she had a lot on her plate. There were reports to review, strategies to plan, and decisions to make. But beyond the numbers and spreadsheets, Monica was also a mother, a wife, a daughter, and a friend. Some days, she felt stretched too thin, wondering if she was really making an impact.

Then she remembered Deborah.

Deborah was not just a prophetess—she was a judge, a leader, and a counselor. She settled disputes, guided a nation, and led an army to victory. In a time when women had few leadership roles, she stood as a beacon of wisdom, courage, and faith.

But what made Deborah remarkable was not just her leadership—it was her ability to balance her many roles. The Bible doesn't tell us that she abandoned her home or neglected her responsibilities. She was

still the “wife of Lappidoth,” meaning she managed her household while also holding court under the Palm of Deborah.
Monica smiled. If Deborah could lead an entire nation while remaining faithful to her calling, surely God could help her navigate her responsibilities too.

Lesson Learned:
Many women today juggle multiple roles—career, home, relationships, and ministry. The pressure can feel overwhelming, but Deborah teaches us that God equips those He calls.
Here’s how Deborah led effectively:

- ✓ She listened to God first – She was a prophetess before she was a leader. Her decisions were rooted in faith, not fear.
- ✓ She sought wisdom in every situation – People came to her because she was known for her godly judgment.
- ✓ She empowered others – She didn’t try to do everything alone; she encouraged Barak to step up and lead.
- ✓ Deborah’s story reminds us that being a leader doesn’t mean doing everything—it means doing the right things with God’s wisdom.

Reflection Questions:

1. *In what ways are you leading at work or at home?*
2. *How can you seek God’s wisdom in your daily decision-making?*
3. *Are there areas in your life where you need to delegate instead of trying to do everything alone?*

Action Plan for the Day:

- ✓ Spend five minutes in prayer, asking God to give you wisdom in your leadership roles today.
- ✓ Identify one responsibility you can delegate to someone else. Don't carry the weight alone!
- ✓ Encourage another working woman today. Send a message, pray for her, or offer words of support.

Prayer:

Lord, thank You for Deborah's example of strength, wisdom, and faith. Teach me to lead with confidence, not in my own strength, but in Yours. Help me to make wise decisions, balance my responsibilities, and encourage others along the way. Fill me with the courage to step into my calling and trust You fully. In Jesus' Name, Amen.

DAY 3: Lydia – The Entrepreneur Who Supported Ministry
(Excelling in Business While Honoring God)

Scripture:
"One of those listening was a woman from the city of Thyatira named Lydia, a dealer in purple cloth. She was a worshiper of God. The Lord opened her heart to respond to Paul's message. When she and the members of her household were baptized, she invited us to her home. 'If you consider me a believer in the Lord,' she said, 'come and stay at my house.' And she persuaded us." – **Acts 16:14-15 (NIV)**

Devotional Story:
The aroma of fresh coffee filled the air as Michelle stepped into her boutique. She had built her fashion business from the ground up—long hours, sleepless nights, and sacrifices that only an entrepreneur could understand. Yet, despite her success, something in her heart was stirring.

That morning, she had read about Lydia, a businesswoman in the Bible. Lydia wasn't just any merchant—she was a dealer in purple cloth, a luxurious and highly sought-after material. She was successful, influential, and well-connected. But what made her stand out wasn't just her business skills—it was her faith.

The Bible describes her as a worshiper of God even before she met Paul. Her success did not distract her from her devotion. When she heard Paul's message, her heart was immediately open, and she was baptized. But Lydia didn't stop there—she used her resources to support ministry, inviting Paul and his companions to stay in her home. She saw her wealth as a means to serve the Kingdom.

Michelle leaned against the counter, reflecting. Was she using her business for God's glory? Sure, she paid her employees well and donated to charity occasionally, but was she truly dedicating her success to God?

Lydia's story reminded Michelle that her business was more than just a source of income—it was a platform for influence, a mission field, and a tool for God's work.

Lesson Learned:

Lydia teaches us that our work and worship are not separate—they go hand in hand. She was successful, but she never let her business become her identity. Instead, she used it to bless others and advance God's mission.

We can do the same. Whether you run a business, work a corporate job, or manage a home, your work is your ministry. When you dedicate it to God, He will use it for His glory.

Reflection Questions:

1. *How do you see your work as a part of God's plan?*
2. *In what ways can you honor God through your business or career?*
3. *How can you use your resources to support ministry and help others?*

Action Plan for the Day:

- ✓ Pray over your work today. Ask God to help you see it as part of His greater plan.
- ✓ Find a way to bless someone with your resources—whether financially, with your time, or through mentorship.
- ✓ If you own a business, consider how you can use it to serve God's Kingdom, just as Lydia did.

Prayer:

Lord, thank You for the example of Lydia, a woman who excelled in business yet remained faithful to You. Help me to see my work as a mission field, a place where I can reflect Your light. May I use my success to serve You and bless others. Keep my heart focused on You, so that in all I do, I bring glory to Your Name. In Jesus' Name, Amen.

DAY 4: Esther – Courage in the Corporate World
(Taking Bold Steps in a Challenging Workplace)

Scripture:
"For if you remain silent at this time, relief and deliverance for the Jews will arise from another place, but you and your father's family will perish. And who knows but that you have come to your royal position for such a time as this?" – **Esther 4:14 (NIV)**

Devotional Story:
Sophia took a deep breath as she walked into the conference room. She was about to present an ethical concern to the board—something that could cost her position but could also save hundreds of employees from unfair policies. She felt the weight of the moment. Would she have the courage to speak up?

She thought of Esther, a young Jewish woman who found herself in a powerful but challenging position. She had been chosen as queen—not through ambition, but through divine placement. Yet when her people faced annihilation, she had to decide whether to remain silent or take a bold stand.

Her cousin Mordecai's words echoed in her mind: "Who knows but that you have come to your position for such a time as this?"

Sophia closed her eyes briefly and whispered, "God, if You put me here, give me the strength to speak."

Like Esther, she knew this moment wasn't about personal ambition or self-preservation—it was about

using her influence for righteousness, even at great risk.
She took another deep breath, stepped forward, and began to speak.

Lesson Learned:
Esther's story reminds us that our positions—whether in the workplace, business, or leadership—are not accidental. God places us where we are for a purpose.
Courage isn't the absence of fear; it's choosing faith over fear. Esther had every reason to stay silent—she could have been killed for approaching the king uninvited. Yet, she stepped forward in obedience, trusting that God would take care of the outcome.
Today, we face different but equally significant decisions. It might be standing up for integrity at work, advocating for someone in need, or making a bold move that honors God. Whatever it is, God calls us to be courageous.

Reflection Questions:

1. *Have you ever been in a situation where you needed to take a stand for what was right?*
2. *How can you trust God to give you boldness in your workplace or business?*
3. *What does it mean for you to be in your position "for such a time as this"?*

Action Plan for the Day:

- ✓ Pray for courage in the workplace. Ask God to help you stand for what is right.
- ✓ Identify one area where you need to speak up, make a decision, or take a bold step.

- ✓ Encourage another woman today who may be struggling with fear in her workplace.

Prayer:

Father, thank You for placing me where I am for a purpose. Like Esther, help me to recognize the moments where I must stand for truth and righteousness. Fill me with courage to speak, act, and move in faith. I trust that You are in control, and I surrender my fears to You. Strengthen me to be a light in my workplace, knowing that I am here "for such a time as this." In Jesus' Name, Amen.

DAY 5: Huldah – A Woman of Wisdom in a Male-Dominated World
(Being a Voice of Knowledge and Discernment)

Scripture:
"So Hilkiah the priest, Ahikam, Akbor, Shaphan, and Asaiah went to speak to the prophet Huldah, who was the wife of Shallum son of Tikvah, the son of Harhas, keeper of the wardrobe. She lived in Jerusalem, in the New Quarter. She said to them, 'This is what the Lord, the God of Israel, says…'" – **2 Kings 22:14-15 (NIV)**

Devotional Story:
Jennifer sat at the boardroom table, surrounded by men who had dismissed her expertise for years. She had worked tirelessly, built her credentials, and earned her place, yet her voice was often overlooked. Today was different. The company was facing a crisis, and the CEO finally asked, "Jennifer, what do you think?"
She took a deep breath, steadied herself, and spoke with wisdom and clarity.
Jennifer's moment reminded her of Huldah, one of the few named female prophets in the Bible. During a time when men dominated leadership and spiritual roles, God chose her to confirm His word. When King Josiah's officials discovered an ancient scroll (later identified as the Book of the Law), they didn't consult the well-known prophets like Jeremiah or Zephaniah. Instead, they sought Huldah.

Huldah was not a queen, a warrior, or a high priest—she was simply a woman filled with the wisdom of God. She spoke truth without hesitation, and her words helped reform an entire nation.

Jennifer realized that day that God doesn't need a title, position, or gender to validate wisdom—He validates His own voice in us. Like Huldah, when we walk in wisdom, people will listen.

Lesson Learned:

Huldah's story teaches us that wisdom is not about gender, age, or status—it is about being attuned to God. She was a voice of truth in a time of spiritual decline, showing that when God speaks through you, even those in high positions will listen.

For women in workplaces dominated by men, Huldah's story is a reminder: your wisdom, discernment, and faithfulness to God are your strength.

Reflection Questions:

1. *Have you ever felt overlooked in your workplace or community? How did you handle it?*
2. *How can you grow in wisdom and discernment like Huldah?*
3. *What steps can you take to make sure your voice is used for God's purposes?*

Action Plan for the Day:

- ✓ Pray for wisdom and confidence to speak when the time is right.
- ✓ Seek God's direction in your work and decision-making today.

- ✓ Encourage another woman who might feel unheard or overlooked.

Prayer:
Lord, thank You for the example of Huldah, a woman of wisdom and boldness. Help me to trust that my voice matters and that You have given me discernment for a purpose. When I feel overlooked, remind me that You see me. Let my words bring truth, clarity, and encouragement to those around me. In Jesus' Name, Amen.

DAY 6: Priscilla – Balancing Work, Ministry & Marriage
(Supporting Family While Making an Impact)

Scripture:
"After this, Paul left Athens and went to Corinth. There he met a Jew named Aquila, a native of Pontus, who had recently come from Italy with his wife Priscilla… Paul went to see them, and because he was a tentmaker as they were, he stayed and worked with them." – **Acts 18:1-3 (NIV)**

Devotional Story:
Rebecca sighed as she looked at the long list of responsibilities in front of her—work meetings, ministry commitments, and making time for her husband. Balancing it all felt impossible.

Then, she read about Priscilla and Aquila. This husband-and-wife duo were not just business partners, but also ministry partners. They worked together as tentmakers and, at the same time, hosted Paul, discipled Apollos, and spread the gospel.

Priscilla was never in competition with her husband. She was a pillar of strength, wisdom, and leadership. She and Aquila made their home a center of ministry while managing their business.

Rebecca smiled. If Priscilla could do it, so could she. Her marriage, career, and faith could work together—if she allowed God to lead.

Lesson Learned:
Priscilla's life reminds us that we don't have to choose between work, family, and faith—God can help us balance it all. She teaches us that when we see work as a calling, marriage as a partnership, and ministry as a lifestyle, everything aligns.

Reflection Questions:

1. *Are there areas in your life where you feel out of balance?*
2. *How can you involve your family in ministry or faith-based activities?*
3. *What adjustments can you make to prioritize what truly matters?*

Action Plan for the Day:

- ✓ Pray with your spouse or a close friend about your work and ministry.
- ✓ Set one small goal to bring better balance into your daily routine.
- ✓ Seek ways to include faith in your work and home life.

Prayer:
Lord, thank You for the example of Priscilla, a woman who managed her work, faith, and marriage with grace. Help me find balance in my own life. Let my work be a testimony of Your goodness, my marriage reflect Your love, and my ministry flow from a place of devotion. In Jesus' Name, Amen.

DAY 7: Sarah – Trusting God's Timing
(Handling Workplace Delays and Personal Disappointments)

Scripture:
"Then one of them said, 'I will surely return to you about this time next year, and Sarah your wife will have a son.' Now Sarah was listening at the entrance to the tent... So Sarah laughed to herself." – **Genesis 18:10-12 (NIV)**

Devotional Story:
Emily stared at the rejection email on her screen. She had prayed, worked hard, and given her best, but the promotion she wanted went to someone else—again.

She thought of Sarah, Abraham's wife, who had waited decades for a promise that seemed impossible. When she overheard the angels tell Abraham that she would have a son, she laughed—not out of joy, but out of doubt.

Sarah's laughter was the laughter of a woman who had waited too long. She had buried her dreams and resigned herself to disappointment. But God's timing was not delayed—it was perfect.

Emily wiped her tears and whispered, "Lord, help me trust Your timing, even when it doesn't make sense."

Lesson Learned:
Sarah's story reminds us that delays are not denials. God's timing is perfect, even when it doesn't align

with our plans. Waiting is hard, but His promises never fail.

Reflection Questions:

1. *Have you ever given up on a dream because it took too long?*
2. *How can you trust God's timing in your career and personal life?*
3. *What has God taught you during seasons of waiting?*

Action Plan for the Day:

- ✓ Surrender your timeline to God in prayer.
- ✓ Write down one delayed dream and ask God to renew your faith.
- ✓ Encourage someone else who is waiting on God's promises.

Prayer:

Lord, I confess that waiting is hard. I often doubt and wonder if You've forgotten me. But I know Your timing is perfect. Help me trust You, even when I don't understand. Let me wait with faith, knowing You always keep Your promises. In Jesus' Name, Amen.

STRENGTH FOR DAILY CHALLENGES

DAY 8: Hannah – Praying Through Workplace Struggles

(Finding Strength Through Prayer in Stressful Times)

Scripture:
"In her deep anguish Hannah prayed to the Lord, weeping bitterly. And she made a vow, saying, 'Lord Almighty, if you will only look on your servant's misery and remember me, and not forget your servant but give her a son, then I will give him to the Lord for all the days of his life…'" – **1 Samuel 1:10-11 (NIV)**

Devotional Story:
Tears welled up in Julia's eyes as she sat at her desk, staring at the email she had just received. The promotion she had worked for, prayed for, and dreamed about had gone to someone else—again. She felt the weight of discouragement press down on her chest.
For months, she had given everything to her job, staying late, meeting deadlines, and exceeding expectations. But despite her hard work, she was overlooked, undervalued, and exhausted from the constant disappointments.
That night, Julia sat on her bed and whispered a desperate prayer. *"God, do You see me? Do You hear me? How much longer must I wait?"*
She thought of Hannah, a woman who knew what it meant to pray through pain. Hannah had longed for a child, but year after year, her prayers seemed unanswered. To make matters worse, she had to

endure Peninnah's taunts—a painful reminder of what she lacked.

But Hannah didn't stop praying. In her deep sorrow, she went to the temple, poured out her heart before the Lord, and made a vow of surrender. She didn't demand; she simply entrusted her desires to God.

In time, God answered her prayer and gave her a son, Samuel, who became one of Israel's greatest prophets.

Julia wiped her tears. Like Hannah, she needed to keep praying. Even when circumstances felt unfair, even when doors seemed closed, she could trust that God saw her, heard her, and had a plan for her.

Lesson Learned:

Hannah's story reminds us that prayer is not just about getting what we want—it's about surrendering to God's plan. In our workplace struggles, discouragement, or unfair treatment, we can either let frustration consume us or take our burdens to God in prayer.

Hannah prayed in her distress, and God not only answered her but gave her a testimony. When we pray through our workplace struggles, we shift our focus from the problem to the One who holds the solution.

Reflection Questions:

1. *What workplace struggles are causing you stress or discouragement right now?*
2. *Have you truly surrendered your career concerns to God in prayer?*
3. *How can you develop a habit of turning to prayer instead of worry?*

Action Plan for the Day:

- ✓ Write down your workplace struggles in a journal and pray over them.
- ✓ Take five minutes today to pray for wisdom, patience, and God's guidance.
- ✓ Encourage a colleague who may be struggling with their own workplace challenges.

Prayer:

Lord, like Hannah, I come before You with a heavy heart. There are times when work feels overwhelming, unfair, and discouraging. But I know that You see me. You hear me. Help me trust that Your timing is perfect, and Your plans for me are good. Strengthen me to keep praying through my struggles, knowing that You will make a way. In Jesus' Name, Amen.

DAY 9: Ruth – Diligence & Hard Work
(Staying Dedicated Despite Difficult Circumstances)

Scripture:
"And Ruth the Moabite said to Naomi, 'Let me go to the fields and pick up the leftover grain behind anyone in whose eyes I find favor.' Naomi said to her, 'Go ahead, my daughter.' So she went out, entered a field and began to glean behind the harvesters. As it turned out, she was working in a field belonging to Boaz…" – **Ruth 2:2-3 (NIV)**

Devotional Story:
Melissa sighed as she pulled into the parking lot of the small diner where she worked. It wasn't her dream job, but it was what she had right now.

She had a college degree and had once dreamed of a high-paying career. But after an unexpected job loss, she found herself here—waiting tables, cleaning up after customers, and barely making ends meet.

It would have been easy to complain, but instead, she decided to show up with a good attitude, work diligently, and trust that God had a plan beyond what she could see.

Melissa thought of Ruth, a woman who faced uncertainty but chose diligence over despair. After losing her husband, she could have returned to Moab to seek an easier life. Instead, she chose to stay with Naomi, journey to a foreign land, and work hard in the fields to provide for them.

Ruth wasn't above menial labor. She humbled herself, worked tirelessly, and God saw her faithfulness. It was in those fields that she caught the attention of Boaz, a man who would become her husband and change her destiny.

Melissa smiled as she wiped down a table. Hard work was never wasted in God's hands. Just like Ruth, she would remain diligent and trust that her faithfulness would lead to something greater.

Lesson Learned:

Ruth's story teaches us that God blesses diligence. She didn't sit around waiting for a miracle—she worked, trusted, and remained faithful in the little things.

Even in less-than-ideal jobs or difficult circumstances, we must give our best, knowing that God sees our efforts. Excellence in small things prepares us for greater things.

Reflection Questions:

1. *Are you facing a situation where hard work feels unnoticed or unappreciated?*
2. *How can you remain diligent even when the job feels beneath your expectations?*
3. *In what ways can you trust God's bigger plan while staying faithful in your work?*

Action Plan for the Day:

- ✓ Commit to doing your best today, even in the smallest tasks.
- ✓ Thank God for the opportunity to work, even if it's not where you want to be yet.
- ✓ Encourage someone else who is struggling with feeling stuck in their job.

Prayer:

Lord, sometimes I struggle to see the purpose in my work. I get frustrated, discouraged, and tired. But I know that You see every effort, every moment of diligence, and every unseen sacrifice. Help me work with excellence, trust Your timing, and remain faithful even in the small things. I believe that You have a greater plan for me. In Jesus' Name, Amen.

DAY 10: Martha – Managing Work Without Losing Focus on God
(Learning to Balance Work and Spiritual Priorities)

Scripture:
"But Martha was distracted by all the preparations that had to be made. She came to Him and asked, 'Lord, don't you care that my sister has left me to do the work by myself? Tell her to help me!' 'Martha, Martha,' the Lord answered, 'you are worried and upset about many things, but few things are needed—or indeed only one. Mary has chosen what is better, and it will not be taken away from her.'" – **Luke 10:40-42 (NIV)**

Devotional Story:
Samantha rushed through her morning routine, packing lunches, responding to emails, and trying to get out the door on time. The demands of work and home life left her constantly exhausted. Even during Sunday services, her mind wandered to pending projects and household chores.

One evening, after another long day, she collapsed onto the couch. Her five-year-old son climbed into her lap and asked, *"Mommy, why are you always so busy?"* His innocent question stung.

She thought about Martha, a woman who also struggled with balancing work and devotion. Martha was known for her hospitality, always making sure things were perfect for her guests. She loved Jesus, but her focus was misplaced. She was so consumed with serving Him that she neglected to sit at His feet and receive His teachings.

When Martha complained that her sister Mary wasn't helping, Jesus gently corrected her. He didn't say that serving was wrong—He simply reminded her that spiritual nourishment was more important than endless tasks.

Samantha realized she had become like Martha, so caught up in life's demands that she neglected what truly mattered. Her work was important, but her soul needed moments of stillness with God.

That night, she decided to make a change. Instead of scrolling through her phone before bed, she opened her Bible. Instead of rushing through prayer, she lingered in God's presence. The world's demands would never stop, but she could choose what to prioritize.

Lesson Learned:

Martha's story teaches us that work is necessary, but it should never replace time with God. Responsibilities will always be there, but our relationship with Jesus should come first. When we take time to sit at His feet, He gives us the wisdom, strength, and peace we need to handle life's demands.

Reflection Questions:

1. *Are you so busy with work that you neglect time with God?*
2. *What distractions prevent you from spending time in His presence?*
3. *How can you create space for God in your daily routine?*

Action Plan for the Day:

- ✓ Set aside at least 10 minutes today to be still in God's presence.
- ✓ Make a conscious effort to pause, breathe, and pray throughout the day.
- ✓ Choose one unnecessary distraction and replace it with time in the Word.

Prayer:

Lord, I don't want to be so consumed with my responsibilities that I neglect time with You. Help me to balance my work without losing sight of what truly matters. Teach me to pause, to listen, and to sit at Your feet, knowing that when I seek You first, everything else falls into place. In Jesus' Name, Amen.

DAY 11: Jochebed – Raising Children While Trusting God
(Managing Motherhood and Work Without Fear)

Scripture:
"When she saw that he was a fine child, she hid him for three months. But when she could hide him no longer, she got a papyrus basket for him and coated it with tar and pitch. Then she placed the child in it and put it among the reeds along the bank of the Nile." – **Exodus 2:2-3 (NIV)**

Devotional Story:
Rebecca sat in her office, staring at the clock. It was nearly 5 PM, and she still had reports to finish. But her mind wasn't on work—it was on her two children at home. Guilt weighed heavily on her heart. She wanted to provide for them, but she also wanted to be present for them. Was she doing enough? Was she making the right choices?

She thought about Jochebed, the mother of Moses. Jochebed faced an unthinkable challenge—her son's very life was at risk. Pharaoh had ordered all Hebrew baby boys to be killed, but she refused to let fear control her. She trusted God and acted in faith.

Instead of surrendering to hopelessness, she hid Moses for three months. When she could no longer keep him safe, she made a waterproof basket and placed him in the Nile, entrusting him to God's care. Her faith led to divine intervention—Moses was rescued by Pharaoh's daughter and eventually became Israel's deliverer.

Rebecca realized that, like Jochebed, she needed to trust God with her children. She couldn't control every outcome, but she could commit her children into God's hands, knowing He had a greater plan for them than she ever could.

That night, instead of letting guilt consume her, she prayed over her children and declared God's promises over their lives. She was not just a working mother—she was a mother of faith.

Lesson Learned:

Jochebed's story reminds us that motherhood and work require faith. We may not always feel like we're doing enough, but when we surrender our children to God, He fills in the gaps. Fear and guilt cannot rule us—trusting in His plan must be our foundation.

Reflection Questions:

1. *Do you struggle with guilt as a working mother?*
2. *In what areas of motherhood do you need to trust God more?*
3. *How can you involve God in the raising of your children?*

Action Plan for the Day:

- ✓ Speak a prayer of blessing over your children today.
- ✓ Release any guilt or anxiety, knowing that God is watching over them.
- ✓ Find one small way to be intentionally present with your children today.

Prayer:

Lord, I surrender my children to You, just as Jochebed did with Moses. I trust that You have a perfect plan for their lives, even when I cannot always be there. Remove my guilt, strengthen my faith, and help me to be both a diligent worker and a devoted mother. In Jesus' Name, Amen.

DAY 12: Mary, Mother of Jesus – Embracing a Divine Calling
(Handling Unexpected Life Changes While Working)

Scripture:
"I am the Lord's servant," Mary answered. "May your word to me be fulfilled." Then the angel left her." – **Luke 1:38 (NIV)**

Devotional Story:
Clara had her life planned out. She had worked hard to earn her promotion, and things were finally falling into place. But then, unexpectedly, she found out she was pregnant. She was excited but also overwhelmed. How would she balance this new season of life with her demanding job? The uncertainty left her anxious, questioning whether she was ready for such a change.

One night, as she lay awake, she thought about Mary, the mother of Jesus. Mary was a young woman with her own plans for the future, but everything changed when the angel Gabriel appeared to her with an announcement that would shake her world. She was chosen to carry the Son of God.

This was not what Mary had expected for her life. She was unmarried and lived in a culture where pregnancy outside of marriage could bring shame and rejection. She had every reason to feel afraid and uncertain. But instead of resisting, Mary responded with faith: *"I am the Lord's servant. May Your word to me be fulfilled."*

Clara realized that, like Mary, she needed to embrace this new season with trust in God. Every unexpected change in life—whether a career shift, a move, or a new family responsibility—could be an opportunity for God's plan to unfold. If He called her to it, He would also equip her for it.

Instead of fearing the unknown, Clara decided to embrace the journey. She knew that just as Mary had the strength to carry out God's plan, she too would be given the strength to navigate this new chapter in her life.

Lesson Learned:

Mary's story teaches us that when life changes unexpectedly, God is still in control. He does not make mistakes, and His timing is always perfect. Instead of resisting change, we can trust that He will provide everything we need to fulfill the calling He has placed on our lives.

Reflection Questions:

1. *Have you ever faced an unexpected life change that made you feel uncertain or afraid?*
2. *How can you shift your perspective to see this change as part of God's plan?*
3. *What steps can you take to trust God more when things don't go according to your plan?*

Action Plan for the Day:

- ✓ Write down one unexpected change in your life and surrender it to God in prayer.
- ✓ Find a Bible verse that reminds you of God's faithfulness and meditate on it throughout the day.

- ✓ Remind yourself that God equips those He calls—trust Him in this season.

Prayer:
Heavenly Father, I surrender my plans to You. Like Mary, I want to trust You even when life takes an unexpected turn. Help me to embrace the changes You bring, knowing that Your plans are always good. Give me peace and strength as I walk through this season. In Jesus' name, Amen.

DAY 13: The Proverbs 31 Woman – Excellence in Every Role
(Being a Role Model at Work and Home)

Scripture:
"She sets about her work vigorously; her arms are strong for her tasks… Charm is deceptive, and beauty is fleeting; but a woman who fears the Lord is to be praised." – **Proverbs 31:17, 30 (NIV)**

Devotional Story:
Angela was exhausted. Between managing her responsibilities at work, taking care of her family, and volunteering at church, she felt stretched thin. She wanted to be an excellent employee, a loving wife, a present mother, and a faithful servant—but was it even possible to do it all?

One evening, while reading her Bible, she came across Proverbs 31, a passage describing a woman who seemed to do everything with grace and excellence. She was hardworking, wise, kind, and strong. She provided for her family, made smart business decisions, and feared the Lord.

Angela was inspired but also overwhelmed. How could she ever live up to this standard? But as she studied the passage more closely, she realized that the Proverbs 31 woman wasn't perfect—she was intentional. She prioritized God, worked diligently, and embraced her roles with joy.

Instead of striving for perfection, Angela decided to focus on faithfulness. She began each morning in prayer, asked God for wisdom, and found joy in the work before her. Slowly, she saw a shift in her

perspective—she wasn't just working, she was serving.
And as she served, God gave her the strength to handle every role with grace.

Lesson Learned:
The Proverbs 31 woman is not about perfection—it's about living with wisdom, diligence, and faith. When we invite God into our work, our home, and our daily tasks, He empowers us to do all things with excellence.

Reflection Questions:

1. *Do you feel pressure to be perfect in every area of life?*
2. *How can you shift your mindset from perfection to faithfulness?*
3. *What is one way you can serve your family or workplace with excellence today?*

Action Plan for the Day:

- ✓ Start your day with prayer, asking God for strength in your roles.
- ✓ Identify one small way to bring joy into your work or home.
- ✓ Let go of unrealistic expectations and focus on being faithful.

Prayer:
Lord, help me to walk in excellence, not by my own strength, but by Yours. I surrender my need for perfection and instead ask for wisdom, diligence, and grace. Let my work and home be a testimony of Your goodness. In Jesus' name, Amen

DAY 14: Zipporah – Protecting Family Values in a Busy Life
(Ensuring Spiritual Leadership at Home)

Scripture:
"At a lodging place on the way, the Lord met Moses and was about to kill him. But Zipporah took a flint knife, cut off her son's foreskin, and touched Moses' feet with it." – **Exodus 4:24-25 (NIV)**

Devotional Story:
Melissa's career was thriving, but her family's spiritual life was suffering. Late meetings, weekend assignments, and constant phone calls left little time for family devotionals or prayer. She told herself she'd make time for it later, but later never seemed to come.

Then one night, her daughter asked, "Mom, why don't we pray together anymore?" Melissa's heart sank.

She thought about Zipporah, the wife of Moses. While Moses was called to lead Israel, Zipporah noticed an important oversight—their son had not been circumcised, a sign of the covenant with God. She could have ignored it, but instead, she took immediate action, ensuring that their family remained in alignment with God's commands.

Melissa realized that spiritual leadership wasn't just her husband's responsibility—it was hers too. If she wanted her children to grow in faith, she needed to be intentional.

That night, she gathered her family and prayed together. It was a small step, but one that would have a lasting impact.

Lesson Learned:

Like Zipporah, we must take spiritual leadership seriously, even in the midst of busy schedules. If we want our families to walk in faith, we must be intentional in creating a godly atmosphere at home.

Reflection Questions:

1. *Are you prioritizing your family's spiritual growth?*
2. *What small steps can you take to bring faith into your home?*
3. *How can you lead by example in your household?*

Action Plan for the Day:

- ✓ Set aside time for family prayer today.
- ✓ Find one way to encourage faith in your children or spouse.
- ✓ Be intentional in making God the center of your home.

Prayer:

Lord, help me to be a spiritual leader in my home. In the midst of my busy life, let me never neglect the faith of my family. Give me wisdom and strength to keep You at the center. In Jesus' name, Amen.

OVERCOMING CHALLENGES WITH GRACE

DAY 15: Rahab – Overcoming a Bad Reputation & Finding Purpose

(Rising Above Past Mistakes and Succeeding)

Scripture:
"But Joshua spared Rahab the prostitute, with her family and all who belonged to her, because she hid the men Joshua had sent as spies to Jericho—and she lives among the Israelites to this day." – **Joshua 6:25 (NIV)**

Devotional Story:
Samantha had spent years trying to escape the shadow of her past. In her younger days, she had made choices she deeply regretted—wrong relationships, bad financial decisions, and a series of mistakes that left her feeling unworthy of a second chance. She had changed her ways, but people around her never let her forget who she once was. It seemed like no matter how much good she did now, her reputation still defined her.
One Sunday, as she sat in church, she heard a sermon about Rahab, the prostitute from Jericho. Samantha leaned in, intrigued. Rahab was not a woman of noble background. She lived a life that many judged as sinful, yet when an opportunity came to change the course of her destiny, she took it.
When two Israelite spies entered Jericho, Rahab saw something in them—hope, a future, a different kind of life. Despite the risks, she hid them and made a deal to save her and her family. Because of her faith and

courage, she not only survived the destruction of Jericho but became part of Israel's history. Incredibly, she later became an ancestor of Jesus Christ Himself (Matthew 1:5).

Samantha felt tears fill her eyes. If God could redeem Rahab, He could redeem her too. Her past did not have to define her. Her faith, courage, and choices today mattered more than the mistakes of yesterday.

From that moment, Samantha decided to live boldly, knowing that God's grace had rewritten her story.

Lesson Learned:

Rahab's story teaches us that God does not define us by our past, but by His purpose for us. No matter what we've done or how others see us, God offers redemption. When we step out in faith, He can transform our failures into testimonies of grace.

Reflection Questions:

1. *Have you ever allowed your past mistakes to define your future?*
2. *How can you trust God's redemption and move forward in faith?*
3. *What steps can you take to build a new reputation based on godly character?*

Action Plan for the Day:

- ✓ Write down one mistake from your past that you've been holding onto. Then, tear up the paper as a symbol of releasing it to God.
- ✓ Speak words of affirmation over yourself, declaring God's grace over your life.
- ✓ Identify one way you can serve others today, showing that your life is now a testimony of God's redemption.

Prayer:

Father, I thank You that my past does not define me—You do. Just as You redeemed Rahab and gave her a new future, I believe that You are doing the same for me. Help me to walk in faith, leaving my old reputation behind, and embracing the purpose You have for me. In Jesus' name, Amen.

DAY 16: Mary & Martha
Work vs. Worship
(Choosing What Truly Matters in a Busy Schedule)

Scripture:
"Martha, Martha," the Lord answered, "you are worried and upset about many things, but few things are needed—or indeed only one. Mary has chosen what is better, and it will not be taken away from her."
– **Luke 10:41-42 (NIV)**

Devotional Story:
Emily loved being productive. Her to-do list was always full, and she took pride in getting things done. Whether at work, home, or church, she was constantly busy—organizing, planning, making sure everything ran smoothly. She was the go-to person for getting things done.

But inside, she often felt empty. Despite all her achievements, she felt disconnected from God. She prayed, but it was rushed. She read her Bible, but only when she had time. Worship felt like an obligation rather than a joy.

One day, while reading Luke 10:38-42, she saw herself in Martha. Martha was serving, preparing meals, and ensuring everything was perfect for Jesus. Meanwhile, Mary simply sat at Jesus' feet, listening to Him. When Martha complained, expecting Jesus to correct Mary, she was surprised by His response:

"Martha, you are worried and upset about many things, but only one thing is needed. Mary has chosen what is better."

Emily suddenly realized something: she had been so busy serving Jesus that she had forgotten to sit with Him. She had been prioritizing tasks over His presence. That day, she made a decision—she would no longer let busyness replace worship.

She started waking up a little earlier just to spend time with God. She blocked out moments in her schedule for prayer. And as she slowed down and sat at His feet, she found the peace she had been missing.

Lesson Learned:

Martha was not wrong for working—her mistake was letting work distract her from Jesus. This story reminds us that our greatest calling is to be in His presence. Busyness is not the same as fruitfulness. When we choose worship over worry, we experience peace and purpose.

Reflection Questions:

1. *Are you so busy doing things for God that you forget to spend time with Him?*
2. *How can you make time for worship in your daily routine?*
3. *What changes do you need to make to ensure Jesus remains the center of your life?*

Action Plan for the Day:

✓ Take 15 minutes today to simply sit in God's presence—no distractions, no requests, just worship.

- ✓ Evaluate your schedule and set aside intentional time for prayer and Bible study.
- ✓ Ask God to help you balance work and worship, ensuring He always comes first.

Prayer:

Lord, I don't want to be so busy that I miss out on what truly matters—time with You. Help me to be like Mary, choosing to sit at Your feet instead of being consumed by tasks. Teach me to balance my responsibilities with worship. I surrender my schedule to You. In Jesus' name, Amen.

DAY 17: Eve – Learning from Mistakes
(Avoiding Workplace Temptations and Distractions)

Scripture:
"When the woman saw that the fruit of the tree was good for food and pleasing to the eye, and also desirable for gaining wisdom, she took some and ate it. She also gave some to her husband, who was with her, and he ate it." – **Genesis 3:6 (NIV)**

Devotional Story:
Sophie had always been a hardworking employee, known for her dedication and strong work ethic. She prided herself on being someone who made wise decisions, but that changed the day a subtle temptation came her way.
It started small—just a few extra minutes added to her lunch break, a slight exaggeration on a project report, a harmless gossip session about a colleague. She convinced herself that these were not real issues—everyone did them. But over time, these little choices began shaping her integrity.
One day, an opportunity arose that challenged her character completely. A client offered her an under-the-table deal—if she "adjusted" some numbers in their report, she would receive a hefty reward. It wasn't outright theft, she reasoned; it was just "helping" a client while benefiting herself.
As Sophie sat in her office, wrestling with the decision, she thought about Eve in the Garden of Eden. The temptation had seemed harmless at first. The fruit looked good,

desirable, and beneficial. Eve wasn't planning to defy God—she was just making a choice that seemed reasonable. But that one choice led to devastating consequences for her, Adam, and the entire world.
Sophie realized she was standing at a crossroads—would she allow a moment of temptation to lead her down a destructive path, or would she walk away?
Taking a deep breath, she closed the email and reported the unethical request to her manager. She chose integrity over temporary gain, wisdom over momentary pleasure. And though it wasn't the easy path, it was the right one.

Lesson Learned:
Temptation often presents itself in subtle ways, just as it did for Eve. It rarely looks dangerous at first—it appears appealing, logical, and even beneficial. But small compromises can lead to major downfalls. One bad decision can have lasting consequences, while one wise decision can protect our future.
Eve's story teaches us that temptation is not just about desire but about trust—do we trust God's way, or do we think we know better?

Reflection Questions:

1. *Have you ever justified a small wrongdoing, thinking it was harmless?*
2. *What distractions or temptations in your workplace challenge your integrity?*
3. *How can you strengthen your ability to resist temptation and stay focused on God's principles?*

Action Plan for the Day:

- ✓ Spend a few minutes identifying any area where you may be compromising your values, even in small ways.
- ✓ Ask God for wisdom and strength to resist distractions.
- ✓ Commit to making choices that honor Him, even when they are difficult.

Prayer:

Lord, I recognize that temptations will always come, but I don't want to make choices that dishonor You. Give me discernment to see through deception, courage to walk away from distractions, and faith to trust Your wisdom above my own. Help me to stand strong in integrity. In Jesus' name, Amen.

DAY 18: Tamar – Justice for the Voiceless
(Standing Strong When Wronged in the Workplace)

Scripture:
"She is more righteous than I, since I wouldn't give her to my son Shelah." – **Genesis 38:26 (NIV)**

Devotional Story:
Naomi had worked at her company for years. She was competent, dedicated, and well-respected. But one day, she found herself at the center of a workplace injustice.

She had been promised a promotion—a role she had worked tirelessly for. But when the announcement came, the position was given to someone less experienced, simply because he had better "connections." Naomi was devastated. She had followed the rules, done everything right, and yet, she was overlooked and dismissed as if her efforts didn't matter.

Her first instinct was to accept defeat. After all, what could she do? The system wasn't fair. But then, she thought of Tamar from Genesis 38.

Tamar was a woman who had been deeply wronged. She had been promised a future, but Judah, her father-in-law, refused to fulfill his obligations to her. She was left abandoned and powerless. Yet, she refused to remain silent. Through wisdom and boldness, she exposed the injustice against her. In the end, Judah was forced to acknowledge that Tamar was more righteous than him.

Naomi realized she could either suffer in silence or stand up for herself. With prayer and courage, she approached senior management, presenting her case with facts and fairness. She advocated not just for herself, but for all employees who faced similar biases.

To her surprise, her voice was heard. While she didn't get the promotion immediately, her actions led to policy changes ensuring fairness in future promotions. She realized that sometimes, justice takes time, but God always honors those who stand for what is right.

Lesson Learned:

Tamar's story is one of courage and persistence. She refused to be a silent victim, and God vindicated her.

Many people face injustices—whether it's being overlooked at work, mistreated, or silenced. But God is a God of justice. When we stand for righteousness, He fights for us. Even when immediate justice seems delayed, God sees our struggles and rewards our faithfulness.

Reflection Questions:

1. *Have you ever experienced unfair treatment in the workplace? How did you respond?*
2. *Are there areas where you need to speak up for yourself or others?*
3. *How can you trust God's justice even when fairness seems delayed?*

Action Plan for the Day:

- ✓ If you are facing injustice, pray for wisdom on how to address it with courage.

- ✓ If you see someone else being treated unfairly, offer support.
- ✓ Commit to being a voice for those who are unheard, knowing that God stands with you.

Prayer:

Lord, You are a God of justice. When I face unfair treatment, help me to respond with wisdom, faith, and courage. Give me the strength to stand up for what is right, even when it is difficult. I trust that You see everything and that You will bring justice in Your perfect time. In Jesus' name, Amen.

TRUSTING GOD AND TAKING ACTION

DAY 19: Anna the Prophetess – Faithfulness in the Waiting

(Trusting God's Promises Through Long Seasons)

Scripture:

"She never left the temple but worshiped night and day, fasting and praying. Coming up to them at that very moment, she gave thanks to God and spoke about the child to all who were looking forward to the redemption of Jerusalem." – **Luke 2:37-38 (NIV)**

Devotional Story:

Miriam had been praying for the same thing for over a decade—a breakthrough in her career. Despite her hard work, every opportunity seemed to slip through her fingers. She watched as her colleagues advanced, while she remained stuck in the same role.

She wrestled with doubt. *Had God forgotten her? Was she supposed to give up?*

One evening, as she poured out her heart in prayer, she stumbled upon the story of Anna the Prophetess. Anna was a woman who had endured years of waiting. Widowed at a young age, she could have let grief consume her. Instead, she dedicated her life to worship, fasting, and prayer.

She waited for decades for the promise of God to be fulfilled. And then, one day, she saw Jesus. The Messiah, the fulfillment of her prayers, was right in front of her. Her patience was not in vain.

Miriam realized that waiting is not wasted when it is spent with God. If Anna could remain faithful for years, surely she could trust God with her career. That night, Miriam surrendered her timeline to God. Instead of focusing on what hadn't happened, she focused on Him.

Months later, an unexpected opportunity opened—one she could never have orchestrated herself. It was as if God had been preparing it all along.

Lesson Learned:

Faithfulness in the waiting season is not about doing nothing—it's about staying connected to God. Anna didn't waste her waiting; she filled it with worship. God honors those who remain faithful, even when the wait seems endless.

Reflection Questions:

1. *Are you waiting for something that feels delayed? How have you been handling the waiting?*
2. *How can you shift your focus from frustration to faithfulness?*
3. *What is one way you can actively worship while waiting on God's promises?*

Action Plan for the Day:

- ✓ Instead of focusing on what hasn't happened, spend time in worship today.
- ✓ List the things God has already done in your life, and thank Him for His faithfulness.

Prayer:

Lord, I trust You in the waiting. Even when things seem delayed, I know You are working behind the scenes. Help me to remain faithful, to worship You instead of worrying. Strengthen my heart as I wait for Your perfect timing. In Jesus' name, Amen.

DAY 20: Abigail – Wisdom & Peacemaking in Workplace Conflict (Managing Difficult People with Grace)

Scripture:
"When Abigail saw David, she quickly got off her donkey and bowed down before David with her face to the ground. She said: 'Pardon your servant, my lord, and let me speak to you; hear what your servant has to say.'" – **1 Samuel 25:23-24 (NIV)**

Devotional Story:
Jessica worked in a highly competitive office, where one of her colleagues, Ryan, was notorious for causing conflict. He had a short temper and often escalated minor disagreements into full-blown arguments. One day, he unfairly accused Jessica of sabotaging a project.

Jessica was furious. She had every right to defend herself aggressively. But before she reacted, she remembered the story of Abigail.

Abigail was married to Nabal, a foolish man, who insulted David and almost brought destruction upon their entire household. Instead of reacting emotionally, Abigail intervened with wisdom and humility. She approached David with grace, diplomacy, and intelligence—and in doing so, she saved countless lives.

Jessica decided to handle the situation differently. Instead of matching Ryan's hostility, she calmly requested a private conversation. She listened, clarified the misunderstanding, and chose her words wisely. To her surprise, Ryan apologized. The tension that could have exploded into workplace chaos was defused.

Jessica learned that wisdom, not aggression, resolves conflict. Like Abigail, she chose grace over reaction, peace over pride.

Lesson Learned:

In moments of conflict, we often want to react emotionally, but wisdom calls us to respond intentionally. Abigail teaches us that a soft answer can turn away wrath and that peacemakers bring honor to God.

Reflection Questions:

1. *How do you typically handle workplace conflict?*
2. *What steps can you take to practice wisdom and peacemaking instead of reacting emotionally?*
3. *Who in your life needs a patient and understanding response from you today?*

Action Plan for the Day:

- ✓ If you are facing conflict, pause before reacting. Pray for wisdom and approach the situation with grace, not frustration.

Prayer:

Lord, give me the wisdom of Abigail in handling conflicts. Help me to respond with grace, wisdom, and understanding. May my words bring peace, not division. In Jesus' name, Amen.

DAY 21: Jael – Stepping Up When Others Won't

(Seizing Opportunities with Boldness)

Scripture:
"Most blessed of women be Jael, the wife of Heber the Kenite, most blessed of tent-dwelling women." – **Judges 5:24 (NIV)**

Devotional Story:
Olivia had never considered herself a leader. She preferred working behind the scenes, letting others take charge. But one day, during an important meeting, the team was faced with a challenge, and no one was stepping up to solve it.

As the silence stretched on, Olivia felt a nudge. You can do this.

She hesitated, then thought about Jael in Judges 4. In a time of war, when everyone expected a man to rise up, it was Jael—a simple woman—who seized the moment. She had no military training, but when the enemy commander, Sisera, fled into her tent, she took bold action, delivering victory to Israel.

Jael didn't wait for permission; she stepped up.

Olivia took a deep breath and spoke up. She presented a solution, and to her surprise, the team agreed. That moment marked a turning point for her—she learned that leadership isn't about titles; it's about boldness.

Lesson Learned:
Sometimes, God calls us to step up when no one else will. Like Jael, we may not feel qualified, but

boldness in the right moment can lead to great victories.

Reflection Questions:

1. *Have you ever held back from stepping up because of fear or self-doubt?*
2. *What opportunities are in front of you that require boldness?*
3. *How can you trust God's strength to empower you for leadership?*

Action Plan for the Day:

- ✓ Be on the lookout for a situation where you can step up. Instead of waiting for permission, trust God and take action.

Prayer:

Lord, help me to be bold like Jael. When opportunities arise, give me the courage to step up and lead. Remove my fear and fill me with Your strength. In Jesus' name, Amen.

BUILDING A LEGACY OF FAITH

DAY 22: Elizabeth – Encouraging Others While Waiting on God
(Uplifting Coworkers While Waiting for Personal Breakthroughs)

Scripture:
"After these days his wife Elizabeth conceived, and for five months she kept herself hidden, saying, 'Thus the Lord has done for me in the days when he looked on me, to take away my reproach among people.'" – **Luke 1:24-25 (ESV)**

Devotional Story:
Rebecca had been waiting for years for a well-deserved promotion. She had worked diligently, mentored her colleagues, and taken on extra responsibilities. Yet, every time an opportunity arose, she was overlooked. Meanwhile, she watched younger, less experienced employees climb the corporate ladder.

She struggled with disappointment. *Why, God? Have You forgotten me?*

One morning, as she read her Bible, she came across the story of Elizabeth. Elizabeth and her husband, Zechariah, were righteous and faithful, yet they had no children. In their culture, barrenness was seen as a disgrace. But Elizabeth continued to serve God, never letting her unfulfilled desire steal her faith.

Then, in her old age, God answered her prayers. She conceived a son—John the Baptist—who would prepare the way for Jesus. Instead of being bitter during her waiting season, Elizabeth remained an encourager. When her young cousin Mary came to her, carrying the Messiah in her womb, Elizabeth was filled with joy. Rather than focusing on her own miracle, she celebrated Mary's blessing and spoke words of life over her.

Rebecca realized she had been so consumed by what she lacked that she had forgotten to encourage those around her. She decided to shift her focus. She started mentoring her younger colleagues with a genuine heart, celebrating their promotions rather than envying them.

Months later, her long-awaited promotion came—unexpected and in a way only God could orchestrate. She learned that faithfulness in waiting is often the key to unlocking God's blessings.

Lesson Learned:

Waiting can be difficult, but it's an opportunity to strengthen our faith and encourage others. Elizabeth didn't let her waiting turn into bitterness—she chose to uplift others. Like Elizabeth, we are called to be cheerleaders for others, even when our own prayers seem unanswered.

Reflection Questions:

1. *How do you handle seasons of waiting? Do you encourage others, or do you let disappointment consume you?*
2. *Can you think of someone around you who is experiencing success? How can you genuinely celebrate and encourage them?*
3. *What would change in your heart if you focused on uplifting others rather than your own waiting?*

Action Plan for the Day:
Find at least one person in your workplace, family, or church to encourage today. Celebrate their success, send them a message, or pray for them.
Shift your focus from what you lack to how you can bless others.

Prayer:
Lord, teach me to wait well. Help me not to become discouraged but to use this season to encourage and uplift those around me. Let my words bring life, just as Elizabeth's did for Mary. Fill me with joy, even as I wait for my own breakthrough. In Jesus' name, Amen.

DAY 23: The Shunammite Woman – Radical Generosity & Trust in God
(Investing in the Lives of Others While Working)

Scripture:
"One day Elisha came to Shunem, and a well-to-do woman was there, who urged him to stay for a meal. So whenever he came by, he stopped there to eat." – **2 Kings 4:8 (NIV)**

Devotional Story:
David had a demanding job in finance. Between deadlines, meetings, and personal responsibilities, he rarely had time for anything outside of work. When his church announced a mission trip to support an orphanage, David felt a tug in his heart, but he hesitated. He told himself, I don't have time. I'm too busy providing for my family.

One evening, he came across the story of the Shunammite woman. She was a wealthy woman who noticed the prophet Elisha passing through her town frequently. Instead of ignoring him, she took the initiative to provide for his needs.

At first, she simply offered him meals. Then, she went a step further and built a room in her house just for him. She didn't ask for anything in return—she gave out of love and faithfulness to God.

David felt convicted. The Shunammite woman was busy with her own responsibilities, yet she made room to invest in others. He realized that generosity isn't about convenience—it's about obedience.

That week, David rearranged his schedule and joined the mission trip. The experience transformed him. He realized that investing in people is never a waste, and God always honors a generous heart.

Lesson Learned:

The Shunammite woman teaches us that true generosity goes beyond convenience. She didn't wait for the perfect time—she saw a need and acted. When we make room for others, we make room for God's blessings.

Reflection Questions:

1. *What are some ways you can be generous in your workplace or community?*
2. *Are you holding back from giving because you feel too busy?*
3. *How can you create space in your life to invest in others?*

Action Plan for the Day:

- ✓ Look for an opportunity to invest in someone today. It could be through your time, finances, or simply lending a listening ear. Don't wait for the perfect moment—act now.

Prayer:

Lord, help me to be like the Shunammite woman. Give me a heart of generosity and a willingness to invest in others, even when life feels busy. Teach me to give without expecting anything in return. In Jesus' name, Amen.

DAY 24: Phoebe – Serving While Leading

(Being a Leader and a Servant at the Same Time)

Scripture:
"I commend to you our sister Phoebe, a servant of the church at Cenchreae, that you may welcome her in the Lord in a way worthy of the saints, and help her in whatever she may need from you, for she has been a patron of many and of myself as well." – **Romans 16:1-2 (ESV)**

Devotional Story:
Ava was a senior manager at a corporate firm, known for her efficiency and leadership skills. Yet, despite her position, she never saw herself as "above" others. She often stayed late to help struggling employees, took time to listen to their concerns, and even stepped in when tasks needed extra hands.
One day, a new intern named Michael was assigned to her team. He was nervous and overwhelmed by the fast-paced environment. Seeing his struggle, Ava didn't scold him or push him aside. Instead, she took time out of her day to guide him, explaining processes and offering encouragement.
At the end of the week, Michael hesitantly asked, "Aren't you too busy to be helping me?" Ava smiled and said, "A good leader doesn't just direct people—they serve them."
This mindset is what made Phoebe such a remarkable figure in the early church. Though not much is written about her, Paul's commendation in

Romans 16:1-2 reveals her as both a leader and a servant. She was a deacon in the church of Cenchreae and a patron, meaning she supported many through financial and practical means. Yet, despite her leadership and influence, she remained a humble servant of the Lord.

Like Ava, Phoebe understood that true leadership is about lifting others up, not elevating oneself. She was entrusted with delivering Paul's letter to the Romans—an incredible responsibility—and she carried it with faithfulness and humility.

Lesson Learned:

Phoebe's life teaches us that servant leadership is the highest form of leadership. In a world where people strive for recognition, God calls us to lead by serving. Whether in the workplace, home, or ministry, our influence is strongest when it is rooted in humility and care for others.

Reflection Questions:

1. *Do you view leadership as an opportunity to serve others, or do you see it as a position of power?*
2. *How can you demonstrate humility and service in your workplace or community today?*
3. *Who has been a servant leader in your life? How did their example impact you?*

Action Plan for the Day:

✓ Find one way to serve someone in your workplace, church, or home today—whether by offering assistance, encouragement, or simply listening. Lead by serving.

Prayer:
Lord, teach me to be like Phoebe. Help me to lead with humility, serve with love, and use my influence to lift others up. Let me reflect Your heart in my leadership. May I never see serving as beneath me, but as my highest calling. In Jesus' name, Amen.

DAY 25: Miriam – Leading Women in Worship & Work

(Leading with Grace and Humility)

Scripture:

"Then Miriam the prophetess, Aaron's sister, took a tambourine in her hand, and all the women followed her, with tambourines and dancing. Miriam sang to them: 'Sing to the Lord, for He is highly exalted. Both horse and driver He has hurled into the sea.'" – **Exodus 15:20-21 (NIV)**

Devotional Story:

Sophia had always been a talented singer and organizer. At her church, she led the worship team and was admired for her ability to inspire people. However, as the team grew, she found herself struggling with pride. She secretly felt that without her, the worship ministry would fall apart.

Then one Sunday, Sophia lost her voice completely. She could not lead worship as she normally did. The team had to step up, and to her surprise, they did beautifully. As she watched them, she realized something powerful: a true leader empowers others rather than seeks the spotlight.

This was a lesson Miriam had to learn as well. She was Moses' older sister, a prophetess, and a leader among the Israelite women. After God parted the Red Sea and delivered Israel from Egypt, Miriam led the women in worship, celebrating God's victory with singing and dancing.

Her leadership was inspiring, but later, she made a critical mistake. In Numbers 12, she and Aaron spoke against Moses, questioning why he had more authority than they did. As a result, God struck Miriam with leprosy for seven days. This humbled her, teaching her that leadership must be rooted in humility, not pride.

Like Sophia, Miriam had great influence, but she had to learn that leadership is not about power, but about glorifying God and guiding others with grace.

Lesson Learned:

Miriam's story reminds us that leadership—whether in worship, work, or ministry—must be carried out with humility and a heart for God. True leaders celebrate others, give God the glory, and never seek to elevate themselves.

Reflection Questions:

1. *Do you seek leadership for personal recognition, or to bring glory to God?*
2. *How can you encourage and empower those around you instead of focusing on your own position?*
3. *What areas of pride do you need to surrender to God in your leadership?*

Action Plan for the Day:

Choose to celebrate someone else's success today. Whether at work, church, or home, take time to recognize and uplift others. A humble leader builds others up.

Prayer:

Father, keep my heart humble in leadership. Let me lead with grace, empowering others instead of seeking my own glory. Like Miriam, may my leadership inspire worship and unity, not pride or division. Teach me to serve You with a pure heart. In Jesus' name, Amen.

FAITH & FINANCES

DAY 26: The Widow of Zarephath – Trusting God in Financial Crisis
(Relying on God in Difficult Financial Situations)

Scripture:
"Then the word of the Lord came to him: 'Go at once to Zarephath in the region of Sidon and stay there. I have directed a widow there to supply you with food.' So he went to Zarephath. When he came to the town gate, a widow was there gathering sticks. He called to her and asked, 'Would you bring me a little water in a jar so I may have a drink?' As she was going to get it, he called, 'And bring me, please, a piece of bread.'"
— **1 Kings 17:8-11 (NIV)**

Devotional Story:
Lisa sat at her kitchen table staring at the pile of unpaid bills. Her bank account was nearly empty, and the thought of feeding her children for the next week seemed impossible. She had done everything she could—cut back expenses, prayed, and even picked up extra shifts. But still, nothing seemed to change.
As she picked up her Bible that evening, she found herself reading about the Widow of Zarephath. This woman, living in a drought-stricken land, was at her breaking point. She had only a handful of flour and a little oil left. Her plan was simple: make one last meal for herself and her son, and then prepare for the worst.
But then Elijah, a prophet of God, appeared and asked her for bread. At that moment, she had to

make a choice—hold onto what little she had or trust that God could provide more. With trembling hands, she obeyed. And God worked a miracle. The flour and oil did not run out until the famine ended.

Lisa closed her Bible, realizing that like the widow, she had been holding onto her fear instead of trusting God's provision. The next morning, she surrendered her worries to God and focused on faith instead of fear. That very day, she received an unexpected call offering her a much-needed financial break.

Sometimes, God's provision comes after we step out in faith. Like the widow, we may be down to our last resources, but when we trust Him, He always makes a way.

Lesson Learned:

God often tests our faith in moments of scarcity. The Widow of Zarephath teaches us that trusting God with our resources invites His supernatural provision. Even when things seem hopeless, God sees, cares, and provides.

Reflection Questions:

1. *In what financial areas do you struggle to trust God?*
2. *How has God provided for you in the past when you had little?*
3. *What steps can you take today to trust God more in your financial situation?*

Action Plan for the Day:

Instead of focusing on financial stress, spend time thanking God for what you do have. Trust that He will provide, and consider blessing someone else today—even in a small way.

Prayer:
Father, I confess that financial struggles often fill me with fear and anxiety. Help me to trust in Your provision like the widow of Zarephath. Give me faith to obey even when I don't see the outcome. I believe that You will take care of me. Thank You for being my Provider. In Jesus' name, Amen.

DAY 27: Susanna – Using Resources to Support God's Work
(Financial Stewardship and Generosity)

Scripture:
"Joanna, the wife of Chuza, the manager of Herod's household; Susanna; and many others. These women were helping to support them out of their own means."
— **Luke 8:3 (NIV)**

Devotional Story:
Karen had always been careful with her finances. She budgeted well, saved for the future, and made sure her family had everything they needed. However, when it came to giving to God's work, she hesitated. She reasoned that she would give when she had extra, but right now, she needed to be wise with her money.
One Sunday, her pastor preached about Susanna—a little-known but incredibly important woman in Jesus' ministry. Unlike the widow of Zarephath, Susanna was not struggling financially. She, along with Joanna and other women, used their resources to support Jesus and His disciples. These women were not preachers or miracle workers, but their financial generosity made Jesus' ministry possible.
Karen realized that she had been viewing giving as an afterthought, instead of a privilege to invest in God's work. She decided to start small—giving consistently, even when it wasn't "extra." Over time, she saw that God not only provided for her needs but multiplied her ability to give.

Susanna's example reminds us that financial stewardship is not just about saving and spending—it's also about giving. When we use our resources for God's kingdom, we become part of something far greater than ourselves.

Lesson Learned:
God blesses us with resources not just for our own comfort, but so that we can bless others and support His work. Whether we have much or little, when we give generously, we partner with God's mission.

Reflection Questions:

1. *Do you view your financial resources as* **yours** *or as something entrusted to you by God?*
2. *How can you use your finances to support God's work in a greater way?*
3. *Have you ever experienced the joy of giving to God's work? What was the result?*

Action Plan for the Day:

✓ Commit to giving intentionally today, whether it's supporting a ministry, blessing someone in need, or sowing into your church. Even if it seems small, trust that God will use it for His glory.

Prayer:
Lord, thank You for the resources You have given me. Help me to be a faithful steward, not hoarding what You have entrusted to me but using it for Your kingdom. Let me give with joy, trusting that You will always provide for my needs. In Jesus' name, Amen.

FAITH IN ACTION

DAY 28: The Canaanite Woman – Bold Faith in the Face of Rejection
(Pushing Forward Despite Challenges at Work)

Scripture:
"Then Jesus said to her, 'Woman, you have great faith! Your request is granted.' And her daughter was healed at that moment." — **Matthew 15:28 (NIV)**

Devotional Story:
Melissa had been in her job for three years, working tirelessly to prove herself. She was skilled, dedicated, and always willing to go the extra mile. Yet, every time an opportunity for promotion arose, she was overlooked. She couldn't help but feel invisible, questioning whether all her hard work was even worth it.

One day, as she poured out her frustration in prayer, she stumbled upon the story of the Canaanite woman. This woman was an outsider—both culturally and religiously. Yet, she refused to let rejection stop her from pursuing what she needed from Jesus.

She had come to Him with a desperate plea: "Lord, have mercy on me! My daughter is suffering terribly." But Jesus did not answer her. Undeterred, she persisted. Even when the disciples wanted to send her away, and even when Jesus told her that His mission was first to Israel, she still refused to back down.

Finally, Jesus tested her faith with a statement that could have discouraged anyone: "It is not right to take the children's bread and toss it to the dogs."

But instead of walking away in defeat, she replied, "Yes, Lord, but even the dogs eat the crumbs that fall from their master's table."

Her faith, boldness, and refusal to accept rejection as final moved Jesus. He responded, “Woman, you have great faith! Your request is granted.” At that moment, her daughter was healed.

Melissa saw herself in this story. She realized that rejection wasn't the end of the road—it was an opportunity to push forward in faith. The Canaanite woman didn't take "no" as the final answer; she pressed on, knowing that God had the power to change her situation.

Encouraged, Melissa refused to be discouraged. She continued working with excellence and faith. Within a few months, an unexpected opportunity arose, one that far exceeded her original hopes. She had learned that persistence in faith brings results.

Lesson Learned:

Rejection does not mean defeat. God rewards bold, persistent faith. Just like the Canaanite woman, we should refuse to give up, even when circumstances seem against us.

Reflection Questions:

1. *Have you ever allowed rejection to stop you from pushing forward?*
2. *What situation in your life requires bold, persistent faith today?*
3. *How can you shift your mindset from defeat to determination?*

Action Plan for the Day:
Instead of seeing rejection as a closed door, view it as a challenge to persist in faith. Take a step today toward something you've been hesitant about. Pray, act, and refuse to give up.

Prayer:
Lord, help me to have the bold faith of the Canaanite woman. When rejection comes, give me the strength to push forward, knowing that You are my provider. I choose to trust You and refuse to be discouraged. Strengthen my faith today. In Jesus' name, Amen.

DAY 29: Dorcas (Tabitha) – Making an Impact Through Good Works
(Using Skills to Bless Others While Working)

Scripture:
"In Joppa there was a disciple named Tabitha (in Greek her name is Dorcas); she was always doing good and helping the poor." — **Acts 9:36 (NIV)**

Devotional Story:
Lisa owned a small tailoring business in her community. She loved her work, but she often felt like what she did was insignificant. She wasn't a preacher or a missionary—just a seamstress making clothes. But deep down, she longed to make a difference.

One Sunday, her pastor preached about Dorcas (Tabitha), a woman in the Bible who made an incredible impact—not by standing on a stage, but by using her skills to serve others.

Dorcas was known for her good works and generosity. She made clothes for widows and the needy, using her talent as a seamstress to bless those around her. She didn't seek recognition; she simply did what she could with what she had.

But her impact was so great that when she died, the community mourned deeply. The widows stood around Peter, showing him the clothes Dorcas had made for them, evidence of her love and kindness. Moved by their grief, Peter prayed and God brought her back to life.

Lisa sat in church, stunned. She had never realized that something as simple as sewing could be a powerful ministry. Inspired by Dorcas, she started sewing for the elderly and single mothers in her town, offering them dignity through beautiful, well-made clothes.

Before long, her small act of kindness began to grow into something greater. People noticed, and her business flourished. What she once saw as an insignificant skill became a tool for impact.

Dorcas reminds us that we don't have to be in the spotlight to make a difference. What matters is how we use what we've been given to serve others.

Lesson Learned:

Every skill and talent can be used for God's glory. Acts of kindness—no matter how small—leave a lasting impact. Like Dorcas, we should use our gifts to serve, uplift, and bless others.

Reflection Questions:

1. *What skills or talents has God given you that can bless others?*
2. *Are you using your gifts to serve, or are you holding back?*
3. *How can you turn your everyday work into an opportunity to make an impact?*

Action Plan for the Day:

- ✓ Look for one way to use your skills or resources to bless someone today. It could be a small act of service, a word of encouragement, or a simple gesture of kindness.

Prayer:
Lord, thank You for the gifts and talents You have placed in me. Help me to see them as tools for Your kingdom. Give me a heart like Dorcas—a heart that serves with love and generosity. May my work, no matter how small, be used for Your glory. In Jesus' name, Amen.

FAITH IN ACTION AND INFLUENCE

DAY 30: Joanna – A Woman of Influence in the Workplace

(Being a Godly Influence in a Secular Workplace)

Scripture:
"Joanna the wife of Chuza, the manager of Herod's household; Susanna; and many others. These women were helping to support them out of their own means." — **Luke 8:3 (NIV)**

Devotional Story:
Joanna walked through the palace halls, her sandals clicking softly against the polished floors. As the wife of Chuza, a high-ranking official in King Herod's court, she had access to the wealth and power of the elite. She dined with nobility, heard the whispers of politics, and lived in luxury.

But while many in her position might have been consumed by prestige, Joanna's heart belonged to Jesus. She had once been tormented by sickness and suffering, but when Jesus healed her, her life changed forever. No longer was she content with the empty rituals of palace life—she longed to be part of something eternal.

Though she remained in Herod's palace, she used her influence and resources to support Jesus' ministry. She did not abandon her world, but instead, she became a quiet yet powerful force for the Kingdom of God right where she was placed.

Imagine the courage it took. King Herod despised Jesus—the same Herod who would later mock Him before His crucifixion. Serving Christ in such an environment was dangerous. Joanna risked her reputation, her marriage, and possibly even her life. Yet, she remained faithful, ensuring that the work of Jesus continued.

In today's world, many Christian women find themselves in workplaces that do not align with their faith. Whether it's corporate offices filled with cutthroat competition or industries where ethics are often compromised, the challenge remains the same: How do we shine the light of Christ in a secular environment?

Joanna teaches us that we don't have to preach to be an influence. Our character, integrity, and generosity speak volumes. She didn't leave the palace—she transformed it by bringing the presence of Jesus into it.

Like Joanna, we are called to use our positions, talents, and resources for God's glory—whether that's through our kindness, our ethical choices, or even our financial support of ministries that spread the Gospel.

Lesson Learned:

God places us in specific environments for a reason. Whether in the palace or in a corporate office, we are called to be salt and light. Our faith should influence our surroundings, not the other way around.

Reflection Questions:

1. *How can you be a positive, godly influence in your workplace?*
2. *Are you using your resources and position to further God's Kingdom?*

3. *What steps can you take to remain strong in your faith while working in a secular environment?*

Action Plan for the Day:

✓ Choose one way to demonstrate Christ's love in your workplace today. It could be through an act of kindness, standing firm in integrity, or encouraging a coworker. Let your faith be seen through your actions.

Prayer:

Father, thank You for placing me in the position I am in today. Help me to be a light in my workplace, just as Joanna was in Herod's palace. Let my words, actions, and character reflect You, and may I use my influence for Your glory. Give me strength to stand firm in my faith, no matter the challenges. In Jesus' name, Amen.

DAY 31: YOU – Walking in Unshakable Faith Every Day
(Living Out Your Calling as a Woman of God)

Scripture:
"And without faith it is impossible to please God, because anyone who comes to Him must believe that He exists and that He rewards those who earnestly seek Him." — **Hebrews 11:6 (NIV)**

Devotional Story:
Mia sat on her bed, staring at the job rejection email on her screen. It was the third one this month. She had prayed, fasted, and done everything she thought she was supposed to do. So why was God silent?
Tears burned in her eyes as she whispered, "Lord, I don't understand. I thought You had a plan for me."
As she sat in the silence, she picked up her Bible and turned to Hebrews 11—the famous "Hall of Faith" chapter. Each verse spoke of men and women who walked in faith:
Noah built the ark before he had ever seen rain.
Abraham left everything he knew, believing in a promise he couldn't yet see.
Moses chose to suffer with God's people rather than enjoy the pleasures of Egypt.
One thing was clear: faith wasn't about seeing—it was about trusting. Every person in that chapter had one thing in common: they believed God even when they couldn't see the outcome.
Mia realized something: faith isn't about getting what you want, when you want it. It's about walking

forward, trusting that God is leading you even when the path is unclear.

She wiped her tears and whispered, "Lord, I will trust You. Even when I don't see the answer yet, I know You are working."

Days turned into weeks, and then, a phone call came. It was an opportunity—one even better than she had originally prayed for. In that moment, she understood: faith is about persistence, not perfection.

Living a life of faith means waking up each day and choosing to trust God no matter what happens. It means believing in His goodness, even when circumstances suggest otherwise.

Lesson Learned:

Faith is not about always understanding **what** God is doing—it's about trusting **who** God is. He rewards those who seek Him, even when the journey feels uncertain.

Reflection Questions:

1. *Have you ever struggled to trust God when things didn't go as planned?*
2. *What areas of your life require you to walk by faith today?*
3. *How can you strengthen your faith when doubt tries to creep in?*

Action Plan for the Day:

Make a faith declaration today. Write down one area where you need to trust God and speak life over it. Pray and believe that He is working—even when you can't see it yet.

Prayer:

Father, thank You for teaching me to trust You, even when I don't understand. Help me to walk in unshakable faith, knowing that You are always working for my good. Strengthen my heart when doubt tries to creep in, and remind me that You are faithful. I choose to believe, no matter what. In Jesus' name, Amen.

Final Words:

You have now walked through the lives of 30 incredible women of faith. But today, the final chapter is about YOU. Your faith journey is still being written. Like Joanna, like Dorcas, like the Canaanite woman—God has called you to something greater.
Will you trust Him? Will you live out your calling with boldness and faith?

Your story is just beginning!

Conclusion

Dear Sister in Christ,

As you reach the final day of this devotional, I pray that your heart has been strengthened, your faith deepened, and your perspective on work and life transformed. Over the past 31 days, we have walked through the stories of remarkable women—some well-known, others often overlooked—but each chosen by God to fulfill His purpose. Their lives were not perfect, their journeys were not easy, but they remained faithful, courageous, and impactful.
Through them, you have learned that:

- ✓ *God is with you in the waiting, the struggles, and the victories.*
- ✓ *Your work—whether in the office, home, or community—is an opportunity to glorify Him.*
- ✓ *Faith and influence go hand in hand. Every task, every conversation, every challenge is a chance to shine His light.*

You may have identified with Martha, trying to balance work and worship. Or perhaps you saw yourself in Abigail, called to be a peacemaker in conflict. Maybe you found inspiration in the Canaanite Woman, who refused to let rejection stop her from pursuing her miracle. Or you admired the Proverbs 31 Woman, striving for excellence in all areas of life.
But here's the most important takeaway from this journey: You, too, are a Woman of Unshakable Faith. God has uniquely placed you where you are, not by accident, but by divine assignment. Whether you lead in boardrooms, manage a home, teach in a

classroom, serve in ministry, or work tirelessly in any other role—your faith matters. Your obedience, kindness, integrity, and perseverance are impacting lives, even when you don't see it.

What Now?

This devotional may be ending, but your journey of faith continues. I encourage you to:

- ✓ *Continue seeking God daily. Keep spending time in His Word, allowing it to guide your steps.*
- ✓ *Apply what you've learned. Whether it's stepping out in boldness like Jael, leading with wisdom like Miriam, or trusting God with your finances like the Widow of Zarephath, take action.*
- ✓ *Be a light wherever you go. Your workplace, home, and community need women like you—women who walk in strength, purpose, and faith.*
- ✓ *Encourage others. Just as Elizabeth uplifted Mary, be a source of support and wisdom to another woman who may need it.*

Final Prayer

Father, I thank You for every woman who has walked through this devotional. May she know that she is seen, loved, and chosen by You. Strengthen her faith, fill her with courage, and guide her steps as she continues to serve You in her work and daily life. May she never doubt her purpose, and may she always walk in the confidence that You are with her. In Jesus' name, Amen.

Sister, you are a Woman of Unshakable Faith. Now go and live it out!

About the Author 'GERARD ASSEY'

Gerard Assey is a Graduate in Economics, a PGD in Management (HRD) and holds a Doctorate in Leadership. Gerard holds several International Qualifications in Sales, Debt Collection, Training & Teaching, and is a 'Fellow' of the prestigious 'Institute of Sales & Marketing Management'-UK, a Certified NLP Practitioner, a 'Certified Trainer', an 'Accredited Management Teacher-Behavioral Sciences', a 'Certified Competency Facilitator', a 'Certified Management Consultant'- (the International credentials of a professional management consultant, awarded in accordance with global standards of the ICMCI); and a Certification from the University of Michigan in 'Successful Negotiation: Essential Strategies and Skills'

He is also a Member of the 'National Association of Sales Professionals' backed with several years experience in varied industries, both in India and Overseas. He also holds an 'Etiquette Consultant' Certification from the USA (by Sue Fox, Author of Best Seller: 'Business Etiquette for Dummies'. She has trained some of the top celebrities' world over). He was also a recipient of a scholarship for extensive training in Japan on 'Corporate Management for India'.

Gerard Assey is 'Founder & Chief Corporate Trainer' of the Group: **'Citius, Altius, Fortius Unlimited'**- an organization that **celebrated 20 years of Glorious Service** in 2021, focusing on 3 Core Competencies:

People. Performance. Profit; in functional areas of Sales & Marketing, HR & Organizational Development, covering Recruitment, Training & Consultancy!

Having managed organizations with large Sales Forces in India & Overseas, his specialization cover extensive areas of Sales Training (All levels - Presentation, Negotiation, Key/ Strategic Accounts Management & Managerial Skills for all sectors), Bid Proposal/ Capture Planning/ Management Trainings, Retail Sales, Customer Service & Customer Retention Programs, Training for Prevention & Collection of Debt, Self & Personal Development Programs (Time Management, Teamwork & Team Building, Business Etiquette & Personal Grooming, Leadership & Managerial Skills, People Management Skills, Train-the-Trainer etc), including preparation of Custom-designed Business Manuals for Internal (HR, Induction, and Sales etc) & External use (Instruction, User Manuals).

Gerard has successfully conducted over 6450 Trainings & Workshops (as of Mar '25) all across India, Middle East, Africa, Europe & S.E. Asia. Besides public programs conducted regularly, both in India & Overseas, he has some of the top names as clients whom he services from Single Owners to large Public & Government undertakings, covering all sectors, for their in-house needs.

His website: www.CollectionSkills.com is the only one in this part of the world to be featured in the 'Collections & Credit Risk Magazine-USA' under 'Who's Who in Training' and ranks TOP, along with other websites listed below on most search engines.

Gerard is author of 181 books already (Mar 2025), all the books being available on all online platforms and outlets as E-books and Paperbacks

A few of our business related books:

1. Bite-sized Bits on Commonsense Management
2. Heart to Heart on Life's Principles'
3. How to become a Successful Manager
4. The Sales Professionals' Master Workbook of S.Y.S.T.E.M.S
5. The Professional Business Email Etiquette Handbook & Guide
6. The Professional Business Video-Conferencing Etiquette Handbook & Guide
7. Professional Presentation Skills
8. Exceptional Customer Service
9. Professional Tele-Marketing Skills
10. Professional Debt Collection Skills
11. The G.R.E.A.T. Sales & Service Workbook
12. Sales Training Advantage for Results (*The Ultimate Sales Training Manual to enable you stand out as a S.T.A.R.*)
13. CEO Daily Planner & Organizer
14. The Sales Professionals' Master Daily Planner
15. The Professional Debt Collector's Master Daily Planner
16. My Daily Planner & Organizer
17. MY EMERGENCY INFORMATION RECORD (Family Emergency & Peace of Mind Planner)
18. The Ultimate Therapist & Counselors Planner and Organizer
19. Building an Ethical Workplace
20. Managing Relationships at Work
21. Managing Business Meetings Effectively
22. Effective Delegation Skills
23. Goal Setting for Success
24. B2B Selling by Email
25. Professional Business Etiquette & Grooming
26. Dining Etiquette & Table Manners
27. Effective Networking Skills
28. Grooming, Etiquette & Manners for Teens, Young Adults & Future Leaders
29. Inter-Personal Skills
30. Get Ready, Get Hired!
31. Selling in a Recession

32. Effective Receivables Management in an Economic Downturn!
33. Real Estate & Property Sales Training
34. Credit Sales & Accounts Receivable Management
35. Selling Skills for Real Estate & Property Advisors
36. Take G.R.E.A.T. C.A.R.E!
37. Spa, Salon & Health Club Selling Skills
38. Selling Travel, Holiday & MICE Services
39. Selling Skills for Spa's, Salons & Health Clubs
40. Retailing in Salons & Spas
41. Selling Holiday, Vacation, Tours & Packages
42. The Power of Sales Referrals
43. Selling Luxury
44. Technical Selling Skills
45. Financial Advisors Sales Training
46. Dealing with Burnout at Work Monopolize Your Markets
47. Selling to Affluent Customers
48. Growing up with Grace
49. Financial Selling Skills
50. *The Effective Manager's Guide: Key Skills to Thrive*
51. From Aspiring to Inspiring: A Guide for New Managers on the Rise
52. The Power of Focus
53. Selling with Integrity: Sell Like Jesus The Perfect Role Model!
54. 31 Habits of Champions: Your 31-Day Journey to Greatness
55. Rejecting Grasshopper Talk: From Grasshopper to Giant-Killer-*Defeating Giants Daily!*
56. Navigate the AI-Powered Future of Bid & Proposals: Up-Skill to Stay Relevant with Alternative Career Paths & Opportunities
57. Hiring Sales Winners
58. Present with Impact
59. Success Unlocked: *Breaking Free from Habits that Hold You Back*
60. Complaints to Cheers, Feedback to Gold: Mastering Complaints Management
61. Thriving Together: *Cultivating Diversity, Equity, and Inclusion*
62. Coaching Skills for Sales Managers

63. Soaring to Success in Business & Leadership: Swifter, Higher, Stronger!
64. From Classroom to Podium: A Student's Guide to Powerful Public Speaking & Presentation Skills
65. Developing Self-Discipline
66. The CEO's 31-Day Power Plan: Unlocking Success through Essential Traits
67. Credibility Matters
68. A Winning Attitude
69. Bid & Proposal Management Using AI
70. Sales Forecasting: A Practical & Proven Guide to Strategic Sales Forecasting
71. Elevate & Energize: *50 Dynamic & Fun Activities for Peak Workplace Morale*
72. 'Sales SOS! Sales on Fire! *30 Days to Conquer Chaos & the Nightmares of Success!'*
73. Mastering Sales Managerial Skills: *Building High-Performing Teams & Driving Exceptional Results*
74. Eagle-Eyed Leadership: Unleashing the Power of 31 Lessons from Eagles
75. The Ultimate Employee Training Guide: *Training Today, Leading Tomorrow*
76. Being More Accountable at Work
77. Creating a Culture of Continuous Improvement
78. Effective Questioning & Listening Skills
79. The Power of Value Selling
80. The Growth Mindset
81. Mastering Professional Help Desk Skills
82. The Power to Lead with Empathy
83. Being Prepared: The Key to Unlocking Success
84. Youthful Spark-Youth Energizers, Activities and Games-Igniting the Fun in Youth
85. Ignite your Motivation for Success
86. Elevate Your Executive Presence: *Your Roadmap to Executive Excellence*
87. Smart Decisions: *Mastering Problem Solving with Strategic Solutions for Business Success*
88. Strategic Planning: *Developing and Implementing Strategic Plans to Achieve Long-Term Business Goals*
89. The Power of Stay Interviews
90. Developing G.R.I.T.
91. Adaptability

92. Diagnosis- *A Key Skill for Leadership*
93. The Burnout-Proof Salesperson: *The Master Guide to Preventing Stress & Burnout*- Strategies for Thriving in Sales
94. Learning from Failure: *Keys to Success*
95. Customer Success Management
96. Overcoming the Killers of Motivation
97. The C-Suite Code: *Mastering Skills for Executive Excellence'*
98. Dealing with Difficult Customers
99. Unlocking Your Potential: Mastering the Top 20 Life Skills for a Brighter Future
100. Nurturing Tomorrow's Leaders: *Essential Soft Skills Every Child Must Learn*
101. Lively & Fun Party Games for Seniors & Elders
102. Role Playing for Sales Champions: From Practice to Performance
103. Fun and Exciting Party Games for Kids
104. Case Studies for Sales
105. Role-Playing for Unbeatable Customer Service
106. Case Studies in Customer Service
107. Case Studies in Winning Negotiations
108. Case Studies in Management & Leadership
109. Case Studies in Human Resources & Talent Management
110. CEO Success Blueprint: The Essential Toolkit for CEOs and C-Level Executives
111. The Salesperson's Self-Coaching Guide: *Master Your Own Self-Coaching Plan for Success*
112. Overcoming Procrastination: *Your Ultimate Guide to Stop Delaying and Start Living Your Best Life*
113. When True Colors Are Exposed: *The Journey to Unmasking Humanity*
114. Life-Changing Habits for Teens: Teen Success Blueprint for a Bright Future
115. Workplace Stress-Free: *Proven Strategies to Thrive at Work and Beyond*
116. Objection Overruled: *The Ultimate Guide to Turning 'No' into 'Yes'*

From the Ministry side, Gerard graduated in the very first batch of Charis Bible College-India & had for over 9 years served as a Part-time Faculty at Charis Bible College-Chennai (Andrew Wommack Ministries-Colorado, USA).
He is also a graduate of the Advanced Mentorship Program (AMP) and the Circle Of Ministerial Engagement (C.O.M.E.) of Prophet Jerome Fernando and a Spiritual Son of the Esteemed Prophet.
An accomplished author of several Secular & Christian Books, Gerard has been on the board of a few international organizations and boasts of being the SON of the MOST HIGH GOD: An ordinary guy following an extraordinary GOD!

...And some of his most recent Christian Books being:

1. A Bouquet of Praises for My KING
2. Christian Jokes for the Serious Religious' Folks!
3. Jesus Healed You!
4. Praise24Ever! (also in Tamil version)
5. The 5G Network of GOD
6. Building Faith over F.E.A.R- FACE EVERYTHING AND RISE with JESUS
7. Hebrew and Greek Praise and Worship Words
8. Godly Mothers' and Grandmothers' Bible Story time for Kids!
9. Miracles of Jesus in Pictures
10. Raise your Praise all 365 Days
11. Thanking GOD with an Attitude of Gratitude
12. Meditating on the Attributes of GOD
13. Puppet Scripts
14. Alcohol Ruins, JESUS Reforms, Renews & Restores!
15. Habakkuk 2:2 Christian Daily Journal, Planner & Organizer
16. ABC of GOD's Word for Handwriting Practice
17. Daily Bible Verse Handwriting Practice (Building Godly Character & Faith through Cursive Handwriting Practice!)
18. Guiding Light: Fun & Faith-Building Bible Activities for Children
19. Rejecting Grasshopper Talk: From Grasshopper to Giant-Killer-*Defeating Giants Daily!*
20. Teen Titans of Faith: *Building Courage, Determination & Christ-like-Esteem*
21. I AM Empowered: *Unleashing Divine Power with Positive Declarations*
22. Be A Solution Provider-*From Passion to Purpose*: *A Biblical Guide to Being the Answer to the World!*
23. Miracles of JESUS

24. Parables of Jesus for a Meaningful Life!
25. A Grateful Heart: Importance of Sharing Testimonies of GOD's Grace
26. Melodies of Worship to JESUS: 31 Songs of Praise & Worship From My Heart to HIS!
27. I AM SO BLESSED!
28. My Daily Cup of Energizer
29. 31 Leadership Lessons *from* Jesus- *The Supreme Leader*
30. Peace Amidst Storms: A Biblical Guide to Conquering S.T.R.E.S.S.
31. Rise Above: 20 Biblical Eagle Lessons for Life's Triumphs
32. Godly Goal Setting: *The FAITHFUL Blueprint for a Purpose-Driven Life*
33. The Profound Attributes of our Mighty GOD: Understanding the 10S's of the Almighty
34. Worship Now, Worship Forever: *A Journey from Earthly Praise to Eternal Glory*
35. Unceasing Praise & Worship: *365 Days to Worship the King*
36. The ROAR Within: *Living with Purpose and Authority through the Power of the Holy Spirit*
37. From Potential to Purpose: Unlocking and Multiplying Your Talents & Gifts for Kingdom Impact
38. Songs from the Heart: *Worshipping GOD in Your Own Tune & Melody*
39. Awakening Praise & Worship: Hebrew & Greek Words to Raise Your Praise
40. Sing a NEW Song to the LORD Everyday: *Daily Devotions of Praise & Worship to Lift Your Heart & Glorify HIS Name*
41. *The* A.R.O.M.A. of True Worship: *Creating Worship That Delights God*
42. Becoming A Kingdom Champion: *Embracing God's Call for a Life of Purpose & Victory*
43. The Busy Businessman's Daily Devotional: 366 Crisp Truths to Start Your Day Strong
44. The Teacher's Heart: *Daily Devotions for Educators*
45. Anchored! *A 31-Day Devotional for Students Facing Life's Challenges*
46. Suddenly! Unlocking Unorthodox Breakthroughs through Unusual Worship
47. Overcoming Adversity: *Lessons from the Bible for Modern Challenges*
48. LORD, Don't do it without me
49. Kingdom Leadership: *Biblical Principles for Modern Leaders*
50. Heartprints of God- *Growing God's Way:* Daily Devotions for Kids

to Shine Bright

51. Send Judah First: Let your Praises Go up First to See the Mighty Move of GOD
52. DIVINE MOMENTS: *Recognizing, Embracing, Preparing, and Walking into Life-Changing Encounters with God*
53. Be a Builder in the Kingdom: *The C.E.M.E.N.T. Guide to Creating a Lasting Legacy*
54. Unshakable: *Pillars of Godly Womanhood* (Pillars of Faith That Changed History)
55. Lead Like a Shepherd: *14 Essential Traits for Pastoral Excellence*
56. The Worship Leader's Arsenal: *Powerful Exhortations to Ignite Thanksgiving, Praise & Worship*
57. Women of UnShakable Faith: *31-Day Devotional for Strength, Purpose & Influence*

Besides regularly contributing to business & trade journals, including international ones such as the 'Creative Training Techniques' and the 'Sales News' of the U.S.A, He is also a member of several prestigious bodies & trade associations, having participated in many Conferences & Workshops in India & Overseas.

Prior to his last assignment of leading & managing a large MNC as head, Gerard had a 3-year stint in the Middle East as a Consultant with a leading British Consultancy Firm.

As the past 'Official Country Representative' for the International Business Award- 'THE STEVIES'-(the business world's own Oscar) for about 4 years- he ensured a few Indian companies that qualify for the same every year!

Gerard can be contacted at:
Email: training@Sales-Training.in,training@CollectionSkills.com
Websites:

www.Sales-Training.in
www.EtiquetteWorks.in
www.CollectionSkills.com
www.RetailSalesTraining.in
www.SalesTrainingIndia.com
www.ManualPreparation.com
www.TrainingWithPuppets.com
www.FirstContactAcademy.com
www.SalesAndMarketingRecruiter.com

Our TRAININGS that can help your team

- ✓ **Sales Effectiveness**: Selling Skills for any Sector: Service/ Logistics/ FMCG Realty/ Insurance & Finance/ Media/ SPA's, Health Clubs & Salons/ Key Account Management, Effective Negotiation Skills/ Bid & Proposal Management Skills/ Retail Sales Training: Any Sector (Auto, Jewelry, Clothing, Luxury etc)
- ✓ **Customer Service Skills**-Complaints Handling & Customer Retention
- ✓ **Debt Prevention & Collection Skills**
- ✓ **Etiquette & Grooming**
- ✓ **Leadership & Managerial Skills**
- ✓ **Self & Personal Development Skills**: Presentation Skills/ Effective Communication Skills/Business Proposal Writing Skills/ Problem Solving & Decision Making Skills/ Empowering Secretaries-The perfect PA! (For Secretaries & PA's)/ Effective Time Management/ Teamwork & Teambuilding/ P.R.I.D.E- **P**ersonal **R**esponsibility **I**n **D**elivering **E**xcellence

www.ingramcontent.com/pod-product-compliance
Ingram Content Group UK Ltd.
Pitfield, Milton Keynes, MK11 3LW, UK
UKHW021340190726
13845UKWH00027B/653

9 788198 569103